HAUNTED HOUSES

AROUND THE WORLD

BY JOAN AXELROD-CONTRADA

CAPSTONE PRESS
a capstone imprint

Snap Books are published by
Capstone, 1710 Roe Crest Drive,
North Mankato, Minnesota 56003.
www.mycapstone.com

Library of Congress Cataloging-in-Publication Data
Names: Axelrod-Contrada, Joan, author.
Title: Haunted houses around the world / by Joan Axelrod-Contrada.
Description: North Mankato, Minnesota : Capstone Press, [2017] | Series: Snap books. It's haunted! | Audience: Ages 8-14. | Audience: Grades 4 to 6. | Includes bibliographical references and index.
Identifiers: LCCN 2016034858| ISBN 9781515738602 (library binding) | ISBN 9781515738688 (ebook (pdf)
Subjects: LCSH: Haunted houses--Juvenile literature. | Haunted places--Juvenile literature.
Classification: LCC BF1475 .A94 2017 | DDC 133.1/22--dc23
LC record available at https://lccn.loc.gov/2016034858

Editorial Credits
Mari Bolte, editor; Kristi Carlson, designer; Wanda Winch, media researcher; Gene Bentdahl, production specialist

Photo Credits: Alamy Images: Hemis, 26, Michael Freeman, 25, Michelle Enfield, 12, Zuma Press Inc., 13; AwesomeShot Studios: Oren Arieli, 20; Dreamstime: Gillmalo, 29, Manamana, cover (bottom); Getty Images: Keystone, 21; McGregor Museum, Kimberley, South Africa, 22; The Myrtles Plantation, 27; Newscom: Danita Delimont Photography/Greg Johnston, 14; Official White House photo by Pete Souza, 6; Shutterstock: AR Pictures, cover (top), A-R-T, calligraphic design, Ed Ziegler, 28, Everett – Art, 19, Fantom666, grunge background, Frederic Legrand – COMEO, 18, HiSunnySky, floral background, Hyena Reality, 5, ilolab, brick wall design, jakkapan, retro frame design, janniwet, ornate frame, Jojoo64, 8, kzww, wood background, Leremy, ornate sign design, LilGraphie, photo corners design, LovArt, globe design, PeterPhoto123, oval frame, pisaphotography, 16, rayjunk, antique frame, revers, keyhole design, spaxiax, stone wall background; SuperStock: Marsden Archive, 10; Wikimedia: Daniel Case, 24

Printed in China.
092016   007892

TABLE OF CONTENTS

TWO BEDROOMS, ONE GHOST

Picture this: You're alone in a dark, haunted house. Suddenly the temperature dips. The lights flicker. The furniture moves—seemingly by itself. You hear rustling sounds all around you. Is it your imagination?

You can no longer believe it's your imagination when a gauzy form takes shape before your eyes. It's a ghost—and it's floating toward you. *Maybe I shouldn't have snuck in through the rear window,* you think. But regrets don't keep the ghost from getting closer. You rush to a window, but it's shut tight. You're trapped. There's no escape.

Sound like a horror movie? Perhaps, but truth can be stranger than fiction. Believers in the **paranormal** think there are forces at work beyond our understanding. **Skeptics**, though, point to scientific reasons as to why houses seem haunted. Floorboards creak with age, not because of a **supernatural** presence. Faulty wiring is the cause of lights blinking on and off, not angry ghosts.

Whether you believe in ghosts or think there's an easy explanation behind haunted places, the houses in this book are all real locations. You get to decide for yourself whether or not they're haunted. That is, if you dare to read on.

More people today report ghost sightings than ever before. Perhaps modern technology makes it easier to pick up paranormal events.

ALBERT EINSTEIN AND GHOSTS

Albert Einstein wrote that energy cannot be created or destroyed. So what happens to a person's life energy when they die? Maybe that energy takes a different form—instead of powering a human body, the energy becomes a ghost.

Skeptics, though, disagree. They believe that energy stored in the body is simply released into the environment after death.

paranormal: having to do with an unexplained event that has no scientific explanation

skeptic: a person who questions things that other people believe in

supernatural: something that cannot be given an ordinary explanation

THE WHITE HOUSE
WASHINGTON, D.C., USA

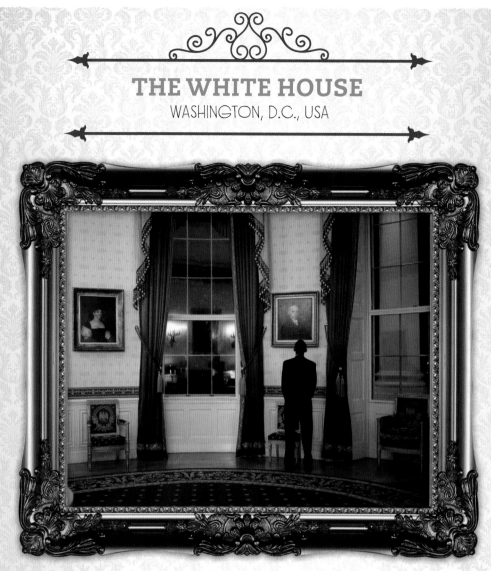

The White House at 1600 Pennsylvania Avenue—the place where the president both lives and works—may be the most famous haunted house in America.

GHOSTS FIT FOR THE PRESIDENT

A history lesson at the White House can quickly turn into a spine-chilling adventure.

Abraham Lincoln, America's 16th president, died on April 15, 1865. Although he's gone, his spirit lives on. He particularly favors the area once used as his office, known today as the Lincoln Bedroom.

Legend has it that former British Prime Minister Winston Churchill encountered Lincoln's ghost during a visit to the White House in the 1940s. Churchill decided to take a late-night bath. He emerged from the tub, only to find Lincoln's ghost standing at the room's fireplace. "Good evening, Mr. President," the prime minister reportedly said. "You seem to have me at a disadvantage."

Never again did he stay in the Lincoln Bedroom.

Other visitors to the White House also report strange happenings. Although he isn't often seen, former U.S. president Andrew Jackson has been heard cursing throughout the White House. First Lady Dolley Madison's phantom lurks around the Rose Garden. During Woodrow Wilson's presidential term, his wife, Ellen, wanted to move Dolley's rose garden. The gardeners assigned to the task were met by Dolley's angry ghost. The roses stayed where they were.

FACT

The ghost of a British soldier from the War of 1812 does not seem to know the war is over. He has been seen wandering the grounds with a torch. One visiting couple said he tried all night to set fire to their bed

BORGVATTNET VICARAGE
BORGVATTNET, RAGUNDA MUNICIPALITY, SWEDEN

Sounds, moving objects, and ghostly shapes have all been
reported at the vicarage.

SPOOKED IN SWEDEN

Borgvattnet Vicarage is known as one of the most
haunted locations in Sweden. New **vicars** arriving at
this humble abode for holy men are quickly acquainted with
the supernatural. The first report of hauntings occurred
in 1927. A **chaplain** on his way to collect his laundry was
surprised to see clothing being pulled off the clothesline by
an invisible force.

Since then people have continued to see paranormal occurrences, including a phantom woman in gray, other ghosts who disappear and reappear, moving objects, and people being forced out of furniture. Some people believe that the ghosts are maids and vicars who have died there.

The vicarage has been a hotel since 1970. The remote location—in a village of about 50 people, five or six hours from the nearest city—is spooky enough for many visitors. Those who make it through the night are awarded diplomas the following morning.

THE OLDER, THE CREEPIER

The older the house, the more likely it is to be haunted. Age gives a place plenty of time for traumatic events to occur. Some victims of tragedy seem unable to move on, so their spirits hang around. The Borgvattnet village dates back to 1750 and the vicarage was built in 1876—so there has been plenty of time to attract spirits.

vicar: a representative of a church

chaplain: a minister, priest, or rabbi who performs religious ceremonies and advises people in the military

BORLEY RECTORY
BORLEY, ESSEX, ENGLAND

Borley Rectory is one of 10,000 haunted locations across the United Kingdom.

A ghostly nun floats through the air. Objects fly across the room. Perfume scents the room. Messages scrawl themselves onto walls. No wonder Borley **Rectory** has been dubbed the "most haunted house in England".

The house was built in 1863 in the village of Borley. But it wasn't the first building on the site. Legend says that the rectory stands on the site of an ancient monastery. A nun fell in love with a monk there, and the two tried to run away together. However, they were quickly found and returned to the monastery. The monk was hanged, and the nun was locked in the monastery cellar forever. Perhaps they could finally be together in death.

The monk and nun were established **specters** by the time the rectory was built. More ghosts made themselves known later. Ghostly faces peered inside the building's new windows. A coach and horses raced up the driveway, only to disappear. A female ghost was even seen during the middle of the day. A dozen clergy refused to live in the abode after hearing eerie tales of hauntings.

In 1940 psychic Harry Price published his book, *The Most Haunted House in England*. He had rented the rectory in 1937 and began a full investigation. He held **séances**, had assistants record unusual sightings, and later even tried to conduct a burial to end the hauntings. The burial was unsuccessful, though—visitors still feel the tug of the supernatural, especially along a pathway called the Nun's Walk.

BEHIND THE HOAX

In 1937 the BBC investigated Borley Rectory and noted more than 2,000 paranormal events. But is the rectory *really* the most haunted house in England?

Not according to Louis Mayerling, a former resident. In 2000 he published a book claiming to explain how some of the more famous "ghost sightings" were faked. Piano strings and ringing bells were plucked or rung by hidden pranksters, not ghosts. Years later, he walked the gardens at dusk in a black cape to look like a scary ghost.

rectory: a building where church leaders live
specter: a ghost
séance: a meeting to contact the spirits of the dead

MOLLY BROWN HOUSE
DENVER, COLORADO, USA

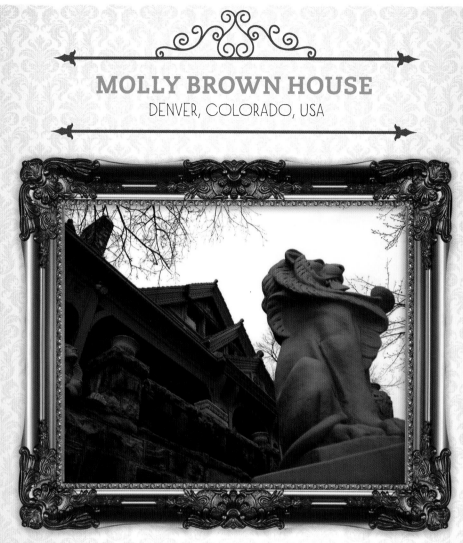

Around 50,000 people visit the
Molly Brown House every year.

Chairs moving by themselves, footsteps crossing the ballrooms, and the smell of phantom pipe tobacco filling the air are only a few of the strange goings-on at the haunted Molly Brown House.

James Joseph "J.J." Brown and his wife, Margaret "Molly" Brown, bought the house in 1894. After Molly survived the sinking of the RMS *Titanic* in 1912, she became known as "The Unsinkable Molly Brown". She and her cigar-smoking husband filled the house with friends and relatives who liked the place so much that they may have decided to stay on as ghosts.

Long-lasting guests are only part of what makes the house spooky. Molly herself has been seen rearranging the dining room chairs. In one room, window blinds raise and lower themselves. The scent of

Ghost hunters use tools that measure electromagnetic fields and energy, temperature, and sounds.

J.J.'s pipe tobacco wafting through the basement and attic is a common occurrence. Molly didn't let J.J. smoke in the house. Maybe he went upstairs or downstairs to light up his pipe in secret. How the scent lingered for more than 100 years remains a mystery.

GHOST HUNTERS

Ghost hunters visit supposedly haunted places. Their specialized, high-tech cameras and recording devices can pick up electronic voice phenomena, or **EVP**, unheard by the human ear.

Other, simpler devices can be used too. Thermometers record sudden drops in temperature, and electromagnetic field (**EMF**) meters mark spikes in EMF signals—the spikes suggest a ghost is visiting. Skeptics, though, dismiss such findings. Changes in the air, they say, come from things such as microwave ovens and bad wiring—not ghosts.

EVP: sounds or voices heard during electronic recordings that can't be explained

EMF: a physical field created by electrically-charged objects

ROSE HALL

MONTEGO BAY, JAMAICA

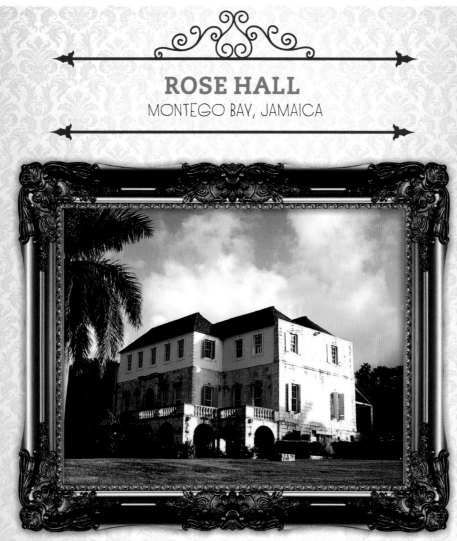

Rose Hall was built in 1770.

From the outside, Rose Hall looks like a mansion in a tropical island paradise. Inside, though, eerie screams echo through the hallways. The White Witch of Rose Hall rests here.

As the story goes, the White Witch began her life as Annie Patterson, born in Haiti to an English mother and Irish father. Annie learned **Voodoo** from her Haitian nanny before moving to Jamaica in the 1820s. She was in search of great wealth—and she found it, marrying plantation owner John Palmer. Rumor says she attracted him with Voodoo.

She quickly became bored with John, who died under mysterious circumstances. Her next two husbands met the same fate.

Annie reportedly enjoyed the company of her male slaves. When she tired of them, they were thrown in the dungeon to die. Legend says that Annie was murdered in her bed by one of those male slaves in the 1830s. But her ghost may have stayed behind to continue her cruel deeds. The mansion is a popular place to hold séances to speak to the dead.

If ever you go to Rose Hall, watch out for the evil cat said to possess Annie's spirit. There is also a portrait of Annie—people say the painting's eyes follow any who pass.

STUBBORN SPIRITS

Sometimes learning why a ghost haunts a certain place is enough to get them to move on. Séances can help paranormal hunters learn why a ghost remains behind. But other times, a spirit will refuse to leave. When that happens, an **exorcism** can be performed to cleanse a house. Some exorcists chant prayers encouraging ghosts to leave. Others use holy water or burn incense and sage leaves.

Even after several sessions, the ghosts may not leave. Some homeowners pack their bags and move. They don't want to risk another brush with the angry ghosts.

Voodoo: a religion that began in Africa; Voodoo is also spelled Vodou

exorcism: a ceremony done to get rid of a spirit

THE TOWER OF LONDON
LONDON, ENGLAND

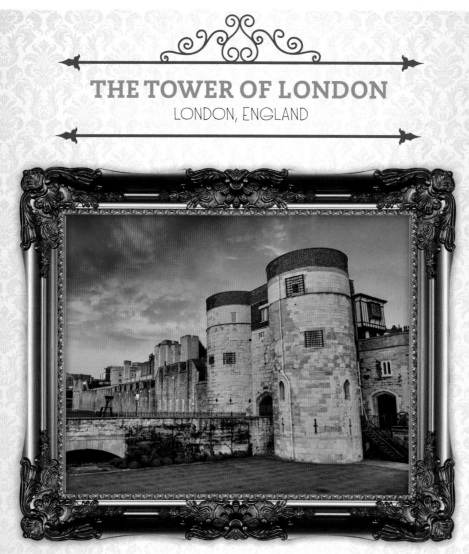

William the Conqueror built the Tower in the early 1080s.

The Tower of London has a fearful reputation as a haunted fortress. Plenty of events worthy of attracting ghosts have occurred over the Tower's thousand-year history.

One of the most mysterious events involves the Princes in the Tower. Twelve-year-old Edward V was ready to take the throne when his father died in 1483. He, and his brother Richard, were sent to the Tower by their uncle. But before the boy king could be crowned, both boys disappeared, leaving their uncle to take the throne. Many believe their uncle, Richard III, was responsible for their deaths.

Visitors have seen the shadows of two young boys, dressed in white, holding each other in fear. The place they haunt is now known as the Bloody Tower—nicknamed because of the princes' mysterious disappearance.

King Henry VIII is famous for having had six wives. Two of them, Anne Boleyn and Catherine Howard, were put to death at the Tower. Anne's headless ghost has been seen in multiple locations. Catherine has been heard pleading for her life.

Henry and Anne's daughter, Queen Elizabeth I, wanted a partnership between the crown and the Protestant religion. During her reign Catholics in England were **persecuted** for their beliefs. When she died in 1603, Catholics hoped that the next ruler, King James I, would leave them in peace. Unfortunately their treatment did not improve.

In 1605 a group of rebels, including a man named Guy Fawkes, put a plan in motion to blow up the Houses of Parliament with a large amount of gunpowder. The king, his wife, and many important Parliament members would be present during the explosion. However, Fawkes and the plotters' plan was discovered before Parliament met. Fawkes was tortured before being hanged, drawn, and quartered at the Tower in 1606. His screams are still heard by visitors to this day.

THE PHANTOM BEAR

There are no real bears in England—but there is a phantom bear! Animals, including bears and lions, prowled the Tower of London for more than 600 years. They were kept in the Royal **Menagerie** as symbols of power and as simple entertainment. Although live bears are no longer kept at the Tower, rumors say the ghost of a bear is still there. One tale says the "grizzly ghost" scared one guard to death.

persecute: to continually treat in a cruel and unfair way

menagerie: a place where animals are kept and trained

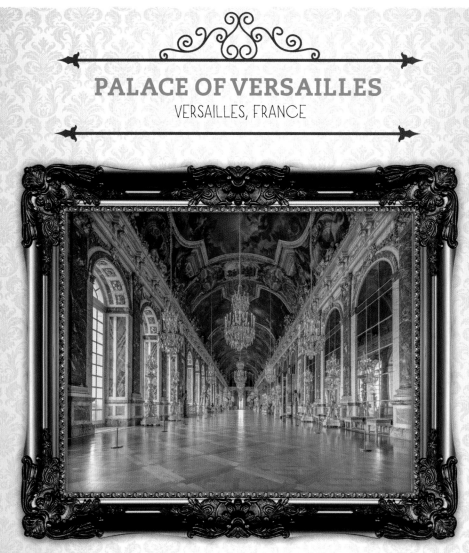

PALACE OF VERSAILLES
VERSAILLES, FRANCE

**King Louis XIV began building the
Palace of Versailles in 1682.**

REVOLUTIONARY GHOSTS

You're visiting the beautiful Versailles Castle, the seat of the French government until 1789. The air grows thick and still. A misty vision of a woman appears. Could it be Queen Marie Antoinette herself?

Yes, if you believe the tale told by two Englishwomen. In *The Adventure*, published in 1911, Annie Moberly and Eleanor Jourdain claimed they traveled back in time to France in the late 1700s.

As their tale goes, they were sightseeing at Versailles and came across people in old-fashioned garb. Then they were warned by a young man to return to the palace. When they did so, they encountered an artist—who they later believed to be the queen.

Skeptics doubt their account. The women didn't write their stories down right away, and they did not see the same things at the same time. When they returned to the palace for a second trip, the layout was completely different than what they claimed to have seen. Believers, though, insist that some people have special powers. Perhaps these people are able to tap into imprints of the past stored in the earth's atmosphere.

Visitors to the old stone buildings of Versailles say they, too, have seen the ghost of Marie Antoinette. In life, the queen built an estate at the palace. Marie broke tradition and customized the estate to fit her own tastes. No one could enter without her personal invitation. Perhaps her ghost has a particularly strong tie to this part of the castle.

Marie Antoinette was beheaded during the French Revolution in 1793.

THE WINCHESTER MYSTERY HOUSE
SAN JOSÉ, CALIFORNIA, USA

There are 160 rooms in the Winchester Mystery House.
Guests can tour 110 of them.

THE GHOST MAZE

The Winchester House has long attracted reports of the paranormal. After the death of her husband and infant daughter, Sarah Winchester contacted a **medium**. The medium told her about a curse on the family. The Winchester rifle had killed thousands of people. He said their spirits wanted revenge. To protect herself, the widow needed to build a new house. She would be safe as long as she never stopped building.

The Winchester House became a twisted maze of hallways, hidden doors, and staircases. Doors opened onto brick walls. Stairs led to nowhere. Sarah believed these random passageways would confuse any ghosts who came after her. To reach her Séance Room, one would have to navigate a series of rooms and hallways. A secret door led to a window that, instead of leading to nothing, was placed at the top of a flight of stairs. At the bottom of the stairs was another stairway that went back up to the previous floor.

Sarah spent much of her time in the Séance Room, holding a séance most evenings. Sometimes she would consult the spirits about building plans. Other times she would ask for protection from evil spirits. She died in 1922. Could her ghost remain behind?

HOW SÉANCES WORK

To conduct a séance, participants first gather in a quiet room. Food, light, and warmth are said to attract the spirits, so candles and savory foods are often present.

At least three people are required for a séance. Everyone sits in a circle and holds hands. Chanting or praying builds the room's energy, drawing spirits to the area. If a spirit responds, participants can ask it simple yes or no questions. When the séance is over, the spirit is thanked and the session ends.

medium: a person who claims to make contact with ghosts

THE RUDD HOUSE
KIMBERLEY, SOUTH AFRICA

Built in the 1870s, the Rudd House is also
known as the Bungalow.

Imagine you are in charge of a historic house. Late at night,
you hear plates crashing in the pantry. Could it be a burglar?
You call the police, but the officer finds nothing. This happens
every night. How long would you last?

The Rudd House sits deep in the heart of South Africa's
diamond country. The Rudd family moved in 1896. Originally
a four-room home, it expanded over time to 22 rooms as the
Rudd families grew.

The daughter-in-law of the first Rudd willed the house to relatives when she died. But, after being spooked by sounds of wailing babies and clanging kitchenware, they refused to live there. They were able to sell the furniture but were unable to find a buyer for the house.

The house is believed to be one of the most paranormally active locations in South Africa. In 1968 it was donated as a museum, restored, and opened to the public in 1988. Since then, no caretaker has lasted longer than six months.

One scholar studied the house for many years. He noticed orbs of light, surrounded by icy air. Ghost hunters believe the icy air in the house comes from ghouls sucking out the energy.

When three journalists sat around the dining table, someone took a picture to record the moment. Only two of the three appear in the photo. Why this is, no one knows.

HOW TO SELL A HAUNTED HOUSE

Do sellers need to tell buyers a house is haunted? Well, it depends on where they live. Laws vary from state to state. Some require sellers to disclose a place's troubled past. However, even if they don't, rumors can spread. Sometimes the address can be changed—but that might not work if it's a distinctive-looking house. Potential buyers can also search to see if a death has occurred in the house.

Some buyers might want to own a haunted house. In 2016 one of the most famous haunted houses, the Amityville Horror house, was listed for $850,000.

CHAONEI NO. 81

CHAOYANGMEN, DONGCHENG DISTRICT, BEIJING, CHINA

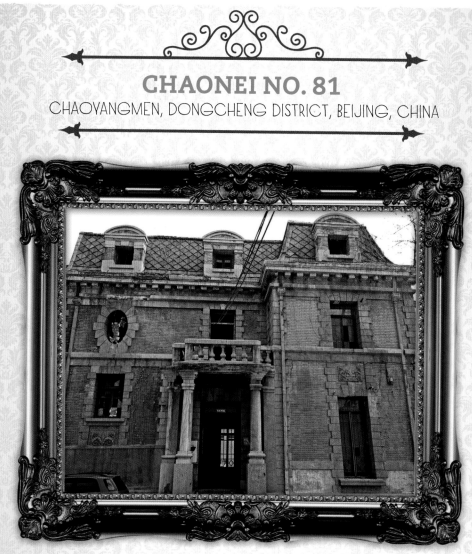

Multi-million-dollar homes go up around Chaonei No. 81, but the building itself remains untouched.

At night, thunderstorms shake the walls of Chaonei No. 81. The deserted house is crumbling, an abandoned shell of a time long past. Those brave enough to approach may hear ghostly cries from within.

In 1949 a civil war in China was at its end. A high-ranking Nationalist soldier, fleeing from the winning Communist army, left his wife behind. Distraught and alone, the woman hanged herself from the mansion's rafters. Her ghostly screams are said to still echo through the vacant, three-story townhouse.

Skeptics say the tale is sketchy. There is no record of a Nationalist soldier and his family living in the home. Regardless of its history, there is something creepy about this 16th century-style home that stands in the middle of gray apartment blocks and modern high rises. Graffiti is scratched into the house's walls, warning visitors to stay away. But, of course, they don't—and maybe the ghosts don't, either.

FACT

During China's month-long Hungry Ghost Festival, restless spirits are thought to prowl the earth. During the festival, the living leave offerings of food and money to their ancestors for use in the afterlife.

Candles, special money, incense, and paper gifts are burned as offerings during the Hungry Ghost Festival.

MYRTLES PLANTATION
ST. FRANCISVILLE, LOUISIANA, USA

Myrtles Plantation represents the style and luxury of the Old South.

Some guests to Myrtles Plantation wake up terrified in the middle of the night and come face-to-face with a ghostly woman in a green headscarf. They may hear a thump, and then a moan. Not many can go back to sleep after a visit from Chloe.

The plantation was built in 1796 by David Bradford, a rebel leader who resisted the U.S. government during the Whiskey Rebellion. When he died, the mansion was sold to his wife's son-in-law, Judge Clark Woodruff, in 1820. Woodruff lived in the grand mansion with his wife and two daughters.

Legend says that Woodruff had secret relationships with several slave girls. One, Chloe, became worried after Woodruff cast her aside. She began eavesdropping to see if he planned to send her away from the house to work the fields. Woodruff caught her, and ordered one of her ears cut off.

In revenge, Chloe poisoned a birthday cake for the Woodruff's daughter. The judge refused a piece, but the children and Mrs. Woodruff ate the cake and died.

The other slaves, worried they'd be blamed for the deaths, hanged Chloe from a tree. Her body was later weighed down and thrown in the river.

These days Myrtles Plantation serves as a bed and breakfast. In 1992 the hazy figure of a slave girl showed up in a photo taken of the mansion. Many believe the ghost is Chloe. Guests also have reportedly seen visions of the Woodruff's daughter at the dining room table. After the tragedy, Woodruff boarded up the room. Could he have trapped his daughter's ghost there forever?

The ghostly shape believed to be Chloe stands between two buildings at the plantation.

ST. AUGUSTINE LIGHTHOUSE
ST. AUGUSTINE, FLORIDA, USA

Today the lighthouse is a museum celebrating the history of St. Augustine.

Mysterious hazy figures, footprints appearing out of nowhere, and moving furniture are just a few supernatural occurrences at the St. Augustine Lighthouse.

Anyone who climbs to the top of this guidepost can feel its tragic past. During the lighthouse's construction in the early 1820s, a group of children were playing on a cart that ran from the lighthouse to the beach. The cart malfunctioned, throwing them into the ocean. Three of the children drowned before they could be rescued. People say their cries for help can still be heard.

In 1859 a keeper fell to his death off the 60-foot (18.3-meter)-high scaffolding he stood on to paint the lighthouse. His death has become part of the tower's legend.

The popularity of ghost hunters brought the lighthouse its fame. In 2005 members of the TV show *Ghost Hunters* recorded a variety of paranormal events, including a mysterious shadow, an otherworldly voice saying, "Help me," and a dark figure leaning over the lighthouse's railing. When viewed under **infrared light**, the figure glowed. The ghost hunters called the tower "the Mona Lisa of paranormal sites."

There are 219 steps leading to the top of the lighthouse.

> **infrared light:** light that produces heat; humans cannot see infrared light

GLOSSARY

chaplain (CHAP-lin)—a minister, priest, or rabbi who performs religious ceremonies and advises people in the military

EMF—a physical field created by electrically-charged objects

EVP—sounds or voices heard during electronic recordings that can't be explained; EVP stands for electronic voice phenomenon

exorcism (EK-sohr-siz-uhm)—a ceremony done to get rid of a spirit

infrared light (IN-fruh-red LITE)—light that produces heat; humans cannot see infrared light

medium (MEE-dee-um)—a person who claims to make contact with ghosts

menagerie (muh-NA-jur-ee)—a place where animals are kept and trained

paranormal (pair-uh-NOR-muhl)—having to do with an unexplained event that has no scientific explanation

persecute (PUR-suh-kyoot)—to continually treat in a cruel and unfair way

rectory (REK-tuh-ree)—a building where church leaders live

séance (SAY-ahns)—a meeting to contact the spirits of the dead

skeptic (SKEP-tik)—a person who questions things that other people believe in

specter (SPEK-tur)—a ghost

supernatural (soo-pur-NACH-ur-uhl)—something that cannot be given an ordinary explanation

vicar (vi-kuhr)—a representative of a church

Voodoo (VOO-doo)—a religion that began in Africa; Voodoo is also spelled Vodou

READ MORE

Doeden, Matt. *The Winchester Mystery House: A Chilling Interactive Adventure.* North Mankato, Minn.: Capstone Press, 2017.

Pearson, Maggie. *Ghosts and Goblins: Scary Stories from Around the World.* Minneapolis: Darby Creek, 2016.

Summers, Alex. *Haunted Houses.* Vero Beach, Fla.: Rourke Educational Media, 2016.

INTERNET SITES

FactHound offers a safe, fun way to find Internet sites related to this book. All of the sites on FactHound have been researched by our staff.

Here's all you do:
Visit *www.facthound.com*
Type in this code: 9781515738602

Check out projects, games and lots more at
www.capstonekids.com

INDEX

READ ALL THE IT'S HAUNTED TITLES!
Titles in This Set